Welcome to the United States of America

Meredith Costain Paul Collins

This edition first published in 2002 in the United States of America by Chelsea House Publishers, a subsidiary of Haights Cross Communications

Chelsea House Publishers
1974 Sproul Road, Suite 400
Broomall, PA 19008–0914

The Chelsea House world wide web address is www.chelseahouse.com

Library of Congress Cataloging-in-Publication Data Applied for.
ISBN 0-7910-6542-1

First published in 2000 by
Macmillan Education Australia Pty Ltd
627 Chapel Street, South Yarra, Australia, 3141

Copyright © Meredith Costain and Paul Collins 2000

Edited by Miriana Dasovic
Text design and page layout by Goanna Graphics (Vic) Pty Ltd
Cover design by Goanna Graphics (Vic) Pty Ltd
Maps by Stephen Pascoe
Illustrations by Vaughan Duck
Printed in Hong Kong

Acknowledgements
The author and the publisher are grateful to the following for permission to reproduce copyright material:

Cover photograph: Hula dancers in Hawaii, © Malvine Roberth.

Meredith Costain pp. 10, 11 (bottom), 22, 26, 30; Blaine Harrington pp. 5–8, 9 (right), 12, 18 (right), 24, 25, 27 (top), 29; AUSCAPE p. 21 (top) © Matthias Breiter-OSF; Pelusey Photography pp. 20, 27 (bottom); Malvine Roberth pp. 9 (left), 11 (top), 13–15, 19, 21 (bottom), 23, 28, 30; Nani Sarpe p. 18 (left).

While every care has been taken to trace and acknowledge copyright the publishers tender their apologies for any accidental infringement where copyright has proved untraceable.

Contents

CANADA

WASHINGTON

OREGON

Rocky Mountains

Theodore Roosevelt
National Park

Missouri River

MINNESOTA

Lake Superior

Niagara Falls

St Lawrence Seaway

Yellowstone
National Park

SOUTH
DAKOTA

Hudson
River

NEVADA

UTAH

Rocky Mountains
National Park

NEBRASKA

Lake
Michigan

Lake
Huron

Lake
Ontario

Detroit

Lake
Erie

New York

San Francisco

Colorado River

Denver

Chicago

Philadelphia

NEW JERSEY

CALIFORNIA

Death
Valley

COLORADO

KANSAS

Mississippi River

Washington DC

MARYLAND

Los Angeles

NEW
MEXICO

OKLAHOMA

Memphis

ARIZONA

Rio Grande River

TEXAS

Atlanta

Atlantic Ocean

Pacific
Ocean

LOUISIANA

Houston

New Orleans

FLORIDA

MEXICO

Gulf of Mexico

Miami

■ Capital city
• Major cities
• Other cities

Arctic Ocean

ALASKA

Yukon River

CANADA

▲ Mt McKinley

N
↑

HAWAIIAN
ISLANDS

Pacific Ocean

Welcome to the USA!

Hi! My name is Erin. I live in Denver, Colorado, in the United States of America, or the USA.

The United States is enormous! It is the fourth-largest country in the world, stretching from the Pacific Ocean in the west to the Atlantic Ocean in the east. We also have borders with Canada in the north and Mexico in the south.

Our country is made up of 50 different states. These include the islands of Hawaii in the Pacific Ocean, and Alaska, which is in the far north near the Arctic Ocean. Because the United States is so big, there are many differences in climate and landscape. Some states are made up mainly of desert or snow-covered wastelands. They have small populations. Other states have big cities with huge populations. Most people in the United States live in **urban** areas.

The United States is a **multicultural** country. The people who live here have **ancestors** who came from all parts of the world. We are a real 'melting pot'!

Family life

Denver is known as the 'Mile High City', because it is a mile, or 1.6 kilometers, above sea level. Although our city is flat, it is on the edge of the towering Rocky Mountains. People come from all over the world to ski at the nearby resorts of Vail and Aspen. We have very cold winters here with lots of snow.

My father's name is Ed. He works as an executive with Union Pacific Railroad. My mother, Beth, works part-time as an accountant for a building contractor. I have one younger sister, Allyson. Grandma Barbara lives with us too. We live in a big, two-story house in the suburbs. There are lots of other young families living in our street.

We have a husky called Tasha. Huskies were once used by the **Inuit** people to pull their sleds across the ice. Tasha loves the snow. Like many huskies, she has one blue eye and one brown one.

Allyson, Tasha, Grandma Barbara and me playing in the snow.

After school and on weekends, I enjoy playing games with my sister and my best friends, Sarah and Erica. In spring and winter, I play soccer. My team is the White Wolves and I play offensive wing. I take gymnastics, read, and sing in our church choir. I like to ski and swim, and I am also a Girl Scout. There are so many things to do in my town!

America is made up of people from many different countries. These children all live in my street. The tall girl at the back is my babysitter, Leah.

School

Children in America start school at the age of five. We go to kindergarten for a year, then move on to elementary school for six years. After that comes three years at junior high, followed by three years at senior high. After graduating from high school, many students go on to another four years at college or university. If students want to become lawyers or doctors, they have to complete even more years at a university.

I travel to school each day on a big, yellow school bus. Our bus driver is called Mr. Jim. He is really nice! My school day starts at 9:05 a.m. and finishes at 3:35 p.m. My subjects include math, science, English, social studies, art, computer lab, library and physical education. My favorite subject is math. I would like to be a teacher when I grow up.

This is my neighbor's kindergarten class. Most American children spend a year or two in kindergarten before they start elementary school.

Sports and leisure

Americans love watching their favorite teams play sports, either from the grandstand or at home in front of the TV. Baseball, football, basketball and ice hockey are the most popular **spectator sports**.

Surfers flock to California and Hawaii for the best waves. Ice-skating, skiing, camping, fishing and mountain-climbing are also very popular. My best friend's parents love to go white-water rafting.

There are lots of youth organizations that help children develop new interests and skills. These include the Girl Scouts and the Boys' Clubs of America. We also have summer camps where we learn skills like survival in the wild, first aid, and search and rescue.

Grid-iron football is one of our most popular sports. Many boys play it at school and college.

Basketball is played everywhere, even in the street!

American culture

The United States is famous for its film industry. American movies such as *Jurassic Park*, *Star Wars* and *Titanic* attract cinema-goers around the world. Our film stars include Humphrey Bogart, Marilyn Monroe, John Wayne, Clint Eastwood, Cameron Diaz and Arnold Schwarzenegger. Walt Disney produced some of the world's best cartoon characters: Mickey and Minnie Mouse, Donald Duck and Goofy. These days, 'The Simpsons' are popular.

Blues and jazz first started in the United States. Blues music is based on the songs sung by black slaves in the southern states. They sang as they worked in the cotton fields. In the 1930s, musicians such as Duke Ellington, Ella Fitzgerald and Dizzy Gillespie, began to play jazz for their friends in city clubs. During the 1950s, musicians such as Chuck Berry and Elvis Presley created a new kind of music. It was called rock'n'roll, and it has influenced popular music across the world ever since.

America has produced many great writers, including William Faulkner, Ernest Hemingway and John Steinbeck. Mark Twain created the characters of Tom Sawyer and Huckleberry Finn, and gave them adventures on the Mississippi River. Our best known **playwrights** are Arthur Miller and Tennessee Williams.

American comics such as 'Superman' and 'Spiderman' are read all over the world.

Young hula dancers in Hawaii. Hawaii is made up of a group of tropical islands in the Pacific Ocean. It became our 50th state in 1959.

Architects such as Buckminster Fuller and Frank Lloyd Wright have left their mark on many American buildings. Our best-known painters include Grandma Moses, who began painting simple scenes of country life at the age of 78, Andrew Wyeth and Georgia O'Keefe. The pop artist Andy Warhol is known for painting everyday items such as tins of tomato soup.

Every year, millions of people visit Graceland, the former home of Elvis Presley. It includes his private car and airplane collection.

Festivals and religion

There is no official religion in the United States. People are free to follow any faith they wish to, or none at all. However, over 60 percent of Americans are Christian. There are more Protestant than Catholic Christians. Other religions practiced include Judaism, Islam and, to a smaller extent, Buddhism and Hinduism.

Religion plays a big part in many people's lives. Church and fellowship groups attract young people from all over the country. Many church-owned television and radio stations broadcast religious programs each day. The Bible is one of the most popular books in America. Around 10 million copies are sold every year.

On Halloween, we dress up as witches or ghosts. Then we visit neighbors, playing 'trick or treat'. They give us candy bars and sweets. We also hollow out pumpkins and carve faces into them. If you put a candle inside the pumpkin, it looks really scary!

Our best-known festival is Independence Day. The whole country gets together to celebrate on the 4th of July every year. The festival marks the Declaration of Independence, adopted on July 4, 1776. This historic document ended British rule.

Thanksgiving is held every year on the fourth Thursday in November. The whole family comes together on this day. We celebrate the end of harvest time and remember the early **settlers** who came to New England nearly 400 years ago. We have a special Thanksgiving Dinner of stuffed turkey, cranberry sauce and pumpkin pie.

American festivals and holidays

New Year	January 1
Groundhog Day	February 2
Valentine's Day	February 14
Saint Patrick's Day	March 17
Labor Day	first Monday in September
Halloween	October 31
Thanksgiving Day	fourth Thursday in November
Christmas	December 25

Christmas lights in New York City.

Food and shopping

You can find food from all over the world in American restaurants and fast-food chains. People love 'fast food' because it is cheap and can be ordered 'out'. This means the food can be taken away and eaten at home. Our most popular fast foods are fried chicken, hamburgers, hot dogs, pizzas and tacos.

Breakfast is an important meal in America. My favorite breakfast is pancakes with scrambled eggs, bacon and sausages, covered in maple syrup! On most mornings, though, I have cereal or toast, and orange juice or milk. I eat a light lunch in the cafeteria at school, and snack on cereal or cookies when I get home. For dinner, we usually have meat and vegetables, or a salad. We finish with dessert. I love ice-cream best.

Many families eat out at restaurants.

Barbecuing is a popular way of cooking food.

In the towns and cities, most supermarkets are open 24 hours a day. They offer a wide variety of fresh food. There are also lots of street markets, selling everything from live chickens to freshly baked sourdough bread.

Every region in the USA has its own specialties. Italian, Spanish and Mexican cooking are popular in California. The ranchers in Texas are famous for their barbecues. In Louisiana, they serve up **jambalaya** and a spicy fish stew called gumbo. KFC, from Maryland, is now known all over the world! We have a long coastline, so seafood is often served in coastal regions. Clam chowder and cooked lobsters, oysters and crabs are popular dishes.

Make July 4th baked beans

This is our favorite dish on Independence Day, although we love to eat it throughout the year!

Ask an adult to help you prepare this dish.

You will need:

- 500 grams (2 cups) navy beans
- I liter (1 quart) water, plus extra water for soaking
- 4 strips bacon
- 1 small can tomato juice
- 50 grams (1/4 cup) ketchup
- 3 tablespoons brown sugar
- 1 onion, chopped
- an oven-proof casserole dish

What to do:

1 Cover beans with cold water and soak overnight.

2 Drain beans and place in a pan with the water.

3 Cut bacon into small pieces and add to beans.

4 Simmer for one hour over low heat.

5 Add tomato juice, ketchup, sugar and onion.

6 Pour the bean mixture into an oven-proof casserole dish.

7 Bake at 200°C (400°F) for two hours.

Make a kite

In summer we love flying kites. They are easy to make, and fun to fly!

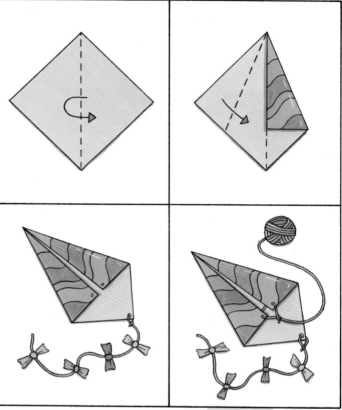

You will need:

- a square piece of paper
- some colored pencils, crayons or felt pens
- a ball of string
- a needle
- 6 pieces of bright tissue paper scraps, each 10 cm by 5 cm (4 in by 2 in)

What to do

1 Draw colorful designs on your piece of paper.

2 Fold the paper to make a triangle. Unfold the paper.

3 Fold two outer edges to the crease.

4 Make three small holes as shown in the diagram.

5 Cut a piece of string, and tie it through the bottom hole of the kite. Crush your pieces of tissue and tie them to the string as shown. This is called the tail string, and is for decoration!

6 Loop the string from the ball through the two holes as shown. Make sure you tie a knot. Do not cut the string from the ball. The string should remain attached to the ball to help you control the kite while it is flying.

A windy day is perfect for kite-flying. Hold your kite in the air and run against the wind. When the wind catches your kite, gradually let out the roll of string. Your kite will fly upside down because the wide end dips down.

Landscape and climate

America's landscape is stunningly beautiful. Our biggest river is the Mississippi River, also known as the 'Father of Waters'. The mighty river starts at Lake Itasca in Minnesota, and winds its way south for 3,780 kilometers (2,350 miles)until it reaches the Gulf of Mexico. The writer Mark Twain called it 'the crookedest river in the world'! Other important rivers are the Missouri, Yukon, Rio Grande, Colorado and Hudson. Our Great Lakes are Michigan, Huron, Ontario, Superior and Erie. If you combined them, they would form the largest area of fresh water in the world.

The spectacular Rocky Mountains stretch from Mexico to Alaska. There are lakes at the base of the mountains that were formed by **glaciers**. In the mid-1800s, gold was discovered here. The Rockies are home to the Grand Canyon, and to the Yellowstone and Rocky Mountain national parks.

The strange desert landscape of Monument Valley, Utah.

Jackson Lake in Grand Teton National Park, Wyoming.

The Great Plains are large, flat, grass-covered areas that stretch from Canada to Texas. There are deserts in south-eastern California, Nevada, Arizona, Utah and New Mexico. Death Valley, which contains a famous national park, is the lowest point in the U.S. It is 86 meters (282 feet) below sea level.

In the desert, temperatures can reach 50°C (122°F) in the shade, and the sun shines for 90 percent of the year! At night, however, it becomes extremely cold. In summer, the high heat levels in the desert cause the air to expand so quickly, and to rise so high, that clouds form and it rains. However, it never rains for long, so the soil is never soaked. After rain, the desert floor becomes awash with color. Flowers blossom everywhere, but they are soon scorched by the hot sun.

Average temperatures

	January	July
Northern states	−14°C to −4°C 7°F to 25°F	18°C to 22°C 64°F to 72°F
Gulf of Mexico states	10°C to 19°C 50°F to 66°F	28°C to 29°C 82°F to 84°F
Desert states	11°C/52°F	33°C/91°F
Central states	−1°C to 2°C 30°F to 36°F	26°C to 28°C 79°F to 82°F

The trees in New England are a blaze of color in autumn.

Plants and animals

About half of the United States was once covered with forests. These were cut down by European settlers who wanted the land for farming. They used the wood for building houses, railways, roads and bridges. Many forest animals lost their homes.

These days, Americans work hard to protect **endangered** plants and animals. There are now hundreds of national parks, forests and monuments to preserve nature and protect wildlife. You can watch buffalo herds grazing in North Dakota's Theodore Roosevelt National Park, or in Yellowstone in Wyoming.

Despite the blazing sun and the heat, the desert is alive with wildlife. Early in the morning you can hear quail, wrens, doves and hummingbirds. In the evening, you might see bald eagles, Harris hawks, or spotted and burrowing owls. There are even roadrunners. They sprint along the ground and use their tails to stop, just as they do in cartoons! Snakes, such as the rattlesnake and sidewinder, live in the desert, too. There are also tarantulas, scorpions, and a type of poisonous lizard called a Gila monster.

Towering Sequoias, or redwoods, in California. These trees can grow to 100 meters (328 feet) and live for hundreds of years.

*Bears in Katmai
National Park,
Alaska.*

Other animals found in this
country include deer, antelopes,
coyotes, bobcats, prairie dogs,
skunks, raccoons and mountain
lions. Squirrels are common
throughout America. They even
live in the parks of densely
populated cities.

*A prairie dog from
Badlands National Park,
South Dakota.*

Cities and landmarks

Our capital city is Washington, **DC**. The city was named after our first president, George Washington. It has wide streets and many fine buildings, including the Capitol and the Lincoln Memorial.

Our busiest city is New York. Over 18 million people live in New York City and its surrounding suburbs. New York is home to the skyscrapers of Manhattan, Wall Street, the Statue of Liberty, the Empire State Building and the World Trade Center. Central Park is an oasis of green in the middle of the city. There are many places to jog, ride horses or to have a picnic.

Los Angeles is the movie capital of the world. Everyone has heard of Hollywood! It offers a great lifestyle. Its mild and sunny climate is ideal for outdoor activities. In Venice Beach and Santa Monica, you can see roller-bladers, artists and body builders on the beaches and boulevards all year.

The giant Statue of Liberty welcomes visitors to America from her position on Liberty Island, in New York Harbor.

The majestic Niagara Falls, on the border of the United States and Canada

San Francisco is famous for the Golden Gate Bridge, Fisherman's Wharf and for its cable cars. Florida is known as the 'Holiday State'. Here you'll find the Everglades, teeming with alligators, snakes and rare birds. Watch out for the mosquitoes!

The Grand Canyon in Arizona is the deepest in the world. It was carved by the Colorado River. The canyon is 445 kilometers (276 miles) long, 1.6 kilometers (1 mile) deep, and reaches 29 kilometers (18 miles) at its widest point.

The heads of four of our presidents are carved into a granite cliff at Mount Rushmore National Memorial, South Dakota. They are George Washington, Thomas Jefferson, Theodore Roosevelt and Abraham Lincoln.

Industry and agriculture

The United States is the biggest trading nation in the world. Americans invented many of the things we use today. These include sewing machines, telephones, computers and planes. Our space program put the first man on the moon in 1969. Brand names such as Ford, General Electric, Coca-Cola, McDonald's, Levi-Strauss and Microsoft are famous all over the world.

More than a quarter of our working people are involved in **manufacturing**. We have large supplies of metals, minerals and oil for our many industries. Over 75 million tons of iron ore are produced each year for our steel mills. Coal is used in steam plants to produce electricity, plastics and synthetics. Oil is found mainly in Alaska and Texas.

Inside the Boeing Aircraft factory in Everett, Washington. Boeing produces over half the planes used by airlines around the world.

A cattle ranch near Rico, Colorado. Beef cattle are our most valuable farm product.

The United States is the largest producer of farm products in the world. Nearly half our land area is farmland. In the 1800s, about 90 percent of Americans worked on farms. These days, only 2 percent work as farmers, and half of them live in the Midwest. Major farming regions include the Corn Belt and the Wheat Belt, southwest of the Great Lakes. California is famous for growing citrus fruit and producing wine.

Fishing is a major industry along the coast and in the Gulf of Mexico. Oklahoma, Texas, Kansas and Nebraska are famous for their ranches and beef cattle. Timber comes from Washington and Oregon, in the northwest.

Transportation

Americans love cars! They are our favorite means of transportation. Most families have at least one car. Our cities and states are linked by a vast network of highways. Many people now choose to live in suburban areas and drive to their jobs in the city. However, having so many cars on the road causes problems, such as traffic jams and **air pollution**.

Buses and trains connect most towns. Our best-known bus line is Greyhound. We have two national train services, Amtrak and Con Rail. Some people prefer to fly when travelling long distances. Our international airlines include American Airlines, Delta Airlines, United Airlines and Northwest Airlines. There are more than 15,000 airports scattered around America. Chicago's O'Hare International Airport is one of the busiest in the world. At peak times, a plane takes off or lands every minute.

A garage in Taos, New Mexico. The car is the most popular way to travel in the United States.

Jets prepare to take off at Newark International Airport, New Jersey.

Ships have been used to move goods since the early days. Today they carry freight from the Atlantic Ocean through the St. Lawrence Seaway, to Great Lake cities such as Chicago and Detroit. Our main seaports are New York City, Houston and New Orleans. Freight is also carried by train or truck.

Streetcars still climb the hilly streets of San Francisco.

History and government

The first people arrived in the country we call America about 20,000 years ago. They came from northern Asia. Some of these people, the ancestors of today's **native Americans**, moved inland. They learned to farm and grow crops. Others, the ancestors of the Inuit, moved to the colder regions in the north.

After Christopher Columbus arrived in 1492, the European settlers came. This spelled disaster for the many tribes of native Americans. Large numbers of them were killed in wars, or died of diseases the settlers brought with them.

Native Americans were the first people to arrive in our country. About 40 different groups once lived on the Great Plains in central United States.

America's early settlers were mainly British. By the mid-1700s, 13 colonies had been set up along the east coast. In 1775, the **colonists** fought against the British in the American War of Independence. They wanted to be free of British rule and British taxes. The Declaration of Independence was signed by the Americans on July 4, 1776. Thirteen years later, George Washington became the first president of the United States.

In 1848, the discovery of gold in California opened up the western part of the country to new settlers. This is where the legends of cowboys and the 'Wild West' began! During 1861–65, the **Civil War** was fought between the northern and southern states. The North won and abolished **slavery**. African-Americans, who had been brought from Africa to work in the cotton fields of the South, were officially now free people.

*Members of the **Congress** meet in the Capitol in Washington, DC.*

The United States has played a key role in the 20th century. We welcomed to our shores large numbers of people from countries all over the world. We were involved in two world wars, as well as the wars in Korea and Vietnam. Many people's lives were affected by the **Great Depression**, and by the collapse of **Wall Street** in 1929. Two of our most famous leaders, Dr. Martin Luther King and President John F. Kennedy, were **assassinated** in the 1960s. However, the people of our country have worked hard to make this one of the most powerful nations in the world today.

Government

The USA is a **federal union** of 50 states. Our national government is based in the District of Columbia, Washington. We are a **democracy**. The president, who is elected by the people, serves a four-year term. No president is allowed to serve more than two terms.

Fact file

Official name United States of America		**Population** 273,000,000	**Land area** 9,373,000 square kilometers (3,655,500 square miles)
Government democracy	**Language** English, but many other languages are spoken too		**Religions** Christianity (Protestants, Catholics) Judaism and Islam
Currency Dollar $1 = 100 cents		**Capital city** Washington, DC	**Major cities** New York, Chicago, Los Angeles, Miami, Atlanta, San Francisco, Denver, Detroit, Philadelphia, Houston
		Climate temperatures vary from bitterly cold in the north, to warm and humid in the south	
Longest river Mississippi 3,780 kilometers (2,350 miles)	**Largest lake** Lake Michigan 57,757 square kilometers (22,525 square miles)	**Lowest point** Death Valley, California 86 meters (282 feet) below sea level	**Highest mountain** Mt McKinley, Alaska 6,193 meters (20,319 feet)
Main farm products corn, wheat, meat, tobacco, fruit and vegetables, fish	**Main industries** manufacturing, cars, electronic and electric equipment, forestry		**Natural resources** oil, coal, iron, natural gas, zinc, copper, silver, timber

Glossary

air pollution	fumes from cars and smoke from factories
ancestors	family members who came before you
assassinated	killed for a political reason
Civil War	a war between the southern (Confederate) states and the northern (Union) states of America. It ran from 1861–1865
colonists	people who settle in a new country
Congress	both houses of the American Parliament (the House of Representatives and the Senate)
DC (Washington)	stands for District of Columbia, to distinguish this city from the state of Washington in the north of the United States
democracy	a government run by the people
endangered	refers to an animal or plant species that is at risk of dying out
federal union	states that are under the control of a central government
glaciers	slow-moving rivers of ice
Great Depression	the period between 1929 and the mid-1930s, when the world economy was in crisis
Inuit	the first people to live in the far north of North America. They were once known as Eskimos
jambalaya	a spicy southern dish made with rice, shrimp and vegetables
manufacturing	the making of goods in factories
multicultural	from many countries
native Americans	the first people to live on the central plains of North America. They were once known as American Indians
playwright	a writer of plays
settlers	people who move to a new place and make it their home
slavery	when people are forced to work without pay
spectator sports	sports that people watch rather than play
urban	in the city
Wall Street	home of the American Stock Exchange

Index